D0345094

CREATIVE RECIPES FOR

TOMATOES

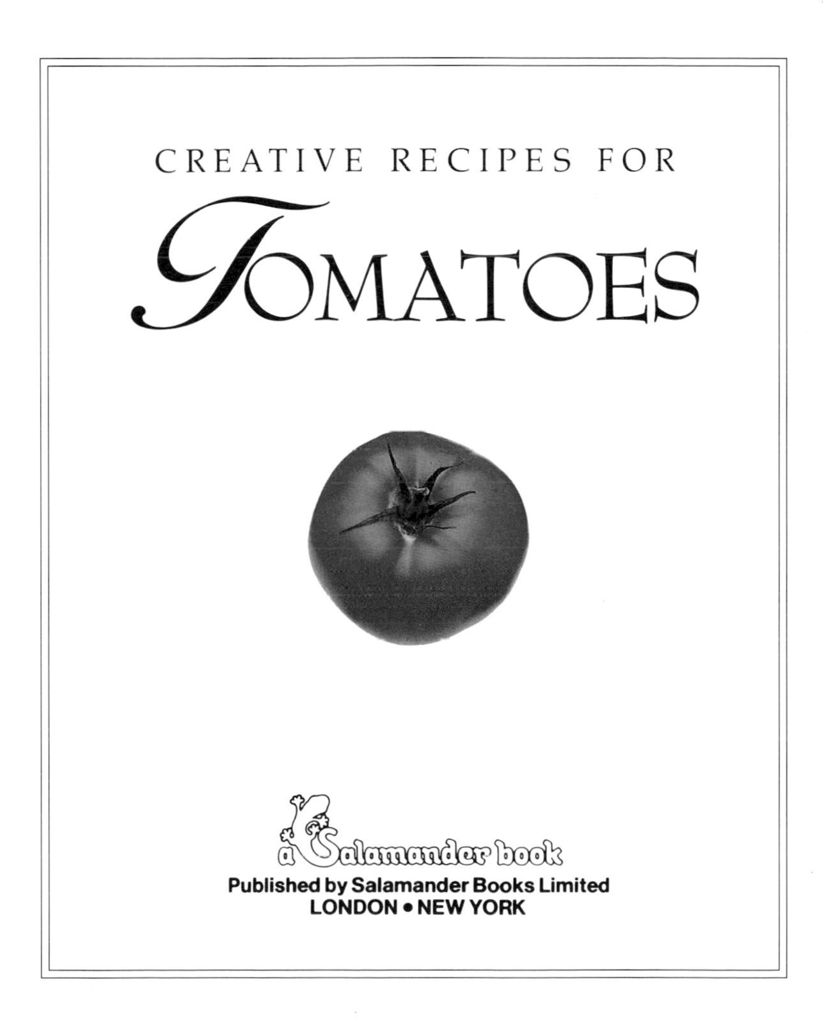

a Salamander book
Published by Salamander Books Limited
LONDON • NEW YORK

Published by Salamander Books Ltd.,
129-137 York Way, London N7 9LG, United Kingdom.

© Salamander Books Ltd., 1991

ISBN 0 86101 603 3

Distributed by Hodder and Stoughton Services, PO Box 6,
Mill Road, Dunton Green, Sevenoaks, Kent TN13 2XX.

All rights reserved. Except for use in a review, no part of this book may be reproduced, stored in a retrieval system or transmitted by any means, electronic, mechanical, photocopying, recording or otherwise, without prior permission of Salamander Books Ltd.

All correspondence concerning the content of this volume should be addressed to Salamander Books Ltd.

CREDITS

RECIPES BY: *Mary Cadogan, Linda Fraser, Kerenza Harries, Janice Murfitt, Cecilia Norman, Lorna Rhodes, and Louise Steele*

PHOTOGRAPHY BY: *David Gill, Paul Grater, Sue Jorgensen, Alan Newnham, Jon Stewart and Alister Thorpe*

DESIGN BY: *Tim Scott*

TYPESET BY: *The Old Mill*

COLOUR SEPARATION BY: *P&W Graphics, Pte. Ltd.*

PRINTED IN BELGIUM BY: *Proost International Book Production, Turnhout, Belgium*

CONTENTS

Summer Tomato Bisque

1 kg (2 lb) ripe tomatoes, chopped
3 spring onions, chopped
½ red pepper (capsicum), seeded and chopped
2 cloves garlic, crushed
500 ml (16 fl oz/2 cups) vegetable stock
1 teaspoon sugar
2 tablespoons chopped fresh basil
60 ml (2 fl oz/¼ cup) crème fraîche or natural yogurt
salt and pepper
1 avocado and snipped fresh chives, to garnish

Put tomatoes, spring onions, red pepper (capsicum) and garlic in a saucepan with stock and sugar.

Bring to the boil, then cover and simmer for 15 minutes. Remove from heat and leave to cool. Purée in a blender or food processor, then sieve into a bowl. Cover and chill for 2 hours. Stir in the basil, crème fraîche or yogurt and add salt and pepper.

Halve avocado and discard stone, peel and slice. Ladle soup into individual bowls, arrange avocado slices on top, then sprinkle with snipped chives and serve. *Serves 6*

GLOBE ARTICHOKES À LA GRECQUE

4 large globe artichokes
2 tablespoons tomato purée (paste)
4 tablespoons olive oil
155 ml (5 fl oz/ ⅔ cup) dry white wine
1 small onion, finely chopped
1 clove garlic, crushed
1 teaspoon chopped oregano
2 sprigs of thyme
2 ripe tomatoes, skinned and chopped
salt and pepper, to taste
lemon wedges and sprigs of oregano, to garnish

Remove stalks and trim outer leaves from artichokes. Rinse well. Cook in boiling salted water for 15 minutes. Drain carefully. Put sauce ingredients into a saucepan, add 155 ml (5 fl oz/ ⅔ cup) cold water, mix well and bring to the boil, then cover and simmer gently for 10 minutes, stirring occasionally. Remove thyme sprigs. Add artichokes to sauce, cover and cook gently for 30 minutes. Remove artichokes and leave to cool. Boil sauce, uncovered, for 5 minutes; leave to cool. Remove chokes by spreading top leaves apart and pulling out the inside leaves. Using a teaspoon, scrape away hairs to expose the heart. Arrange artichokes on plates; spoon sauce around base. Cover and chill. Garnish with lemon wedges and oregano. *Serves 4*

COURGETTE & TOMATO SOUP

30 g (1 oz/6 teaspoons) butter
1 onion, finely chopped
375 g (12 oz) courgettes (zucchini), coarsely grated
1 clove garlic, crushed
625 ml (20 fl oz/2½ cups) vegetable stock
440 g (14 oz) can chopped tomatoes
2 tablespoons chopped fresh mixed herbs, if desired
salt and pepper
60 ml (2 fl oz/¼ cup) double (thick) cream and basil leaves, to garnish

Melt butter in a saucepan, add onion and cook until soft. Add courgettes (zucchini) and garlic and cook for 4-5 minutes.

Add stock and tomatoes with their juice, then bring to the boil, cover and simmer for 15 minutes.

Stir in herbs, if desired, and salt and pepper. Serve the soup in individual bowls, garnished with teaspoonfuls of cream stirred in or floating on the surface and basil leaves. *Serves 4*

TOMATO & MOZZARELLA SALAD

2 beefsteak tomatoes
185 g (6 oz) Mozzarella cheese, sliced
1 small purple onion, thinly sliced
salt and pepper
60 ml (2 fl oz/ ¼ cup) extra virgin olive oil
1 tablespoon fresh basil leaves
1 tablespoon pine nuts

Slice the tomatoes thinly and arrange with slices of cheese, on 4 individual plates. Arrange onion rings on top. Season with salt and pepper, then drizzle oil over the top.

Scatter over the basil and pine nuts and serve at once. *Serves 4 as a main course or 6 as a starter*

TOMATO & ORANGE SOUP

1 orange
3 teaspoons sunflower oil
1 small onion, chopped
1 clove garlic, crushed
750 g (1½ lb) ripe tomatoes, coarsely chopped
500 ml (16 fl oz/2 cups) chicken stock
1 teaspoon sugar
1 teaspoon chopped fresh basil
salt and pepper
60 ml (2 fl oz/¼ cup) double (thick) cream, whipped

Using a potato peeler, cut 4 strips of peel from orange and reserve for garnish. Grate remaining peel and squeeze the juice from orange.

Heat oil in a saucepan, add onion and garlic and cook over low heat for 5 minutes until soft. Add tomatoes and grated peel and cook over medium heat for 5 minutes, until tomatoes become soft. Pour in stock and add sugar and basil, cover and simmer for 15 minutes. Meanwhile, cut reserved orange peel into thin strips and drop into a pan of simmering water for 3 minutes, then drain and carefully dry. Purée soup in a blender or food processor, then press through a sieve. Return to pan and season. Stir in orange juice and reheat gently. Serve with a spoonful of whipped cream in each bowl, topped with orange peel. *Serves 4*

LAMB & WALNUT BITES

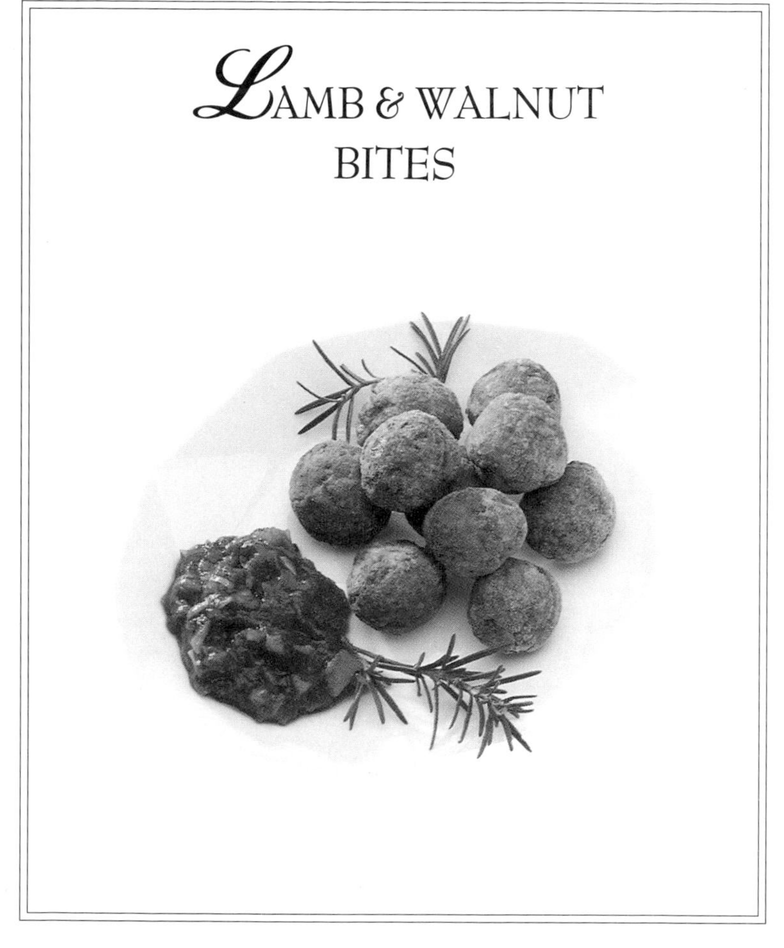

250 g (8 oz) lamb fillet
60 g (2 oz/1 cup) soft breadcrumbs
1 shallot
2 teaspoons fresh rosemary
1 teaspoon salt
½ teaspoon ground black pepper
1 egg
5 pickled walnuts
plain flour
1 onion, finely chopped
1 clove garlic, crushed
3 large tomatoes, peeled, seeded and chopped
3 teaspoons chopped fresh basil
vegetable oil for frying
rosemary or parsley sprigs and cherry tomatoes, to garnish

Finely chop lamb, breadcrumbs, shallot, rosemary, salt, pepper and egg in a food processor until smooth. Dice pickled walnuts. Press a teaspoonful of meat mixture flat, place a piece of walnut in centre and form into a neat ball. Put onion, garlic and tomatoes in a small saucepan and cook rapidly, stirring until thickened. Stir in basil. Half-fill a small pan with oil and heat to 180C (350F). Fry meatballs for 2-3 minutes until golden. Drain. Garnish and serve with sauce. *Makes 35-40*

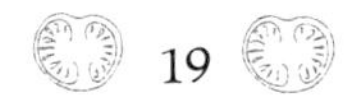

PASTA WITH CLAM SAUCE

1 red pepper
250 g (8 oz/2 cups) strong white flour
pinch of salt
2 eggs, beaten
1 tablespoon olive oil
60 g (2 oz) unsalted butter
1 onion, finely chopped
397 g (14 oz) can chopped tomatoes
pinch of sugar
salt and pepper, to taste
500 g (1 lb) cooked clams, shells removed
2 teaspoons chopped tarragon
3 tablespoons chopped parsley

Grill red pepper until evenly charred. Wrap in foil until cool, then remove skin and seeds. Purée. Sift flour and salt onto a work surface. Make a well, add eggs, oil and red pepper purée, then gradually mix in flour to form a soft dough. Roll out dough thinly, then roll up and cut into strips; set aside. To make sauce, in a pan, melt butter, add onion and soften. Add tomatoes, sugar, salt and pepper and simmer for 20 minutes. Purée and return to pan. Add clams to sauce with herbs; warm through. Cook pasta in boiling salted water for 3-4 minutes; drain well. Serve the pasta topped with the sauce. *Serves 4*

BROCHETTES MEXICANA

375 g (12 oz) trimmed rump steak
375 g (12 oz) pork fillet
1 large red pepper (capsicum), seeded
1 large green pepper (capsicum), seeded
2 fresh green chillies, seeded
250 g (8 oz) can tomatoes
250 g (8 oz) can pimentos, drained
2 tablespoons lemon juice
2 tablespoons olive oil
1 clove garlic, crushed
1 teaspoon turmeric
½-1 teaspoon salt
½ teaspoon pepper

Cut meat into 2.5 cm (1 in) cubes and cut peppers (capsicums) into similar-sized pieces. Purée the marinade ingredients, then simmer in a saucepan until reduced by half. Leave until cold. Stir in meat and peppers (capsicums). Cover and marinate in a cool place for 12 hours.

Thread meat onto skewers, alternating with red and green pepper (capsicum) pieces. Barbecue on rack over hot coals for about 20 minutes, turning frequently and basting with the marinade. Serve with corn or taco chips. *Serves 5-6*

CHICKEN IN SPICY SAUCE

8 chicken thighs, skinned
250 g (8 oz) can tomatoes, drained
6 teaspoons tomato purée (paste)
6 teaspoons chilli sauce
2 teaspoons sugar
3 teaspoons Garam Masala
6 teaspoons light soy sauce
5 cm (2 in) piece fresh root ginger, grated
2 cloves garlic, crushed
juice of 1 lime and 1 lemon
twists of lime and lemon, to garnish

Wash chicken and pat dry with absorbent kitchen paper. Slash meaty parts 2 or 3 times. Place in a shallow non-metal dish.

Put tomatoes, tomato purée (paste), chilli sauce, sugar, Garam masala, soy sauce, ginger, garlic, and lime and lemon juices in a blender or food processor fitted with a metal blade and process until smooth. Pour over chicken, cover and leave in a cool place for 2-3 hours to allow chicken to absorb flavours.

Preheat oven to 190C (375F/Gas 5). Put chicken and sauce in a roasting tin and cook, uncovered, for 45-50 minutes, basting with sauce 2 or 3 times, until tender and cooked. Serve hot, garnished with lime and lemon twists. *Serves 4*

SCALLOPS IN TOMATO CREAM

3 ripe tomatoes, skins removed
500 g (1 lb) shelled queen scallops
1 tablespoon sunflower oil
1 small leek, white part only, finely chopped
4 tablespoons dry vermouth
4 tablespoons dry white wine
155 ml (5 fl oz/⅔ cup) fromage frais
8 basil leaves, torn
salt and pepper, to taste
sprigs of basil, to garnish

Cut tomatoes in half and squeeze out seeds; finely chop flesh. Rinse scallops, removing any dark strands and pat dry with absorbent kitchen paper. In a frying pan, heat oil, add leek and fry gently for about 5 minutes. Add vermouth and wine and bring to the boil, then simmer for 2 minutes. Add scallops, cover and cook for 3-5 minutes, until opaque and firm. Remove with a slotted spoon and keep warm. Boil liquid remaining in pan until reduced to 2 tablespoons. Add tomatoes and heat through. Stir in fromage frais and basil and heat through gently. Season. Spoon the sauce onto 4 warmed serving plates, pile scallops in the centre and garnish with basil. *Serves 4*

*C*LASSIC TOMATO SALAD

500 g (1 lb) firm tomatoes
1 teaspoon sugar
salt and pepper
90 ml (3 fl oz/ 1/3 cup) virgin olive oil
2 tablespoons white wine vinegar
1 tablespoon snipped chives
chopped mixed fresh herbs, to garnish

Slice tomatoes thinly and arrange on a serving plate. Sprinkle with sugar and season with salt and pepper. Mix oil and vinegar together in a bowl or screw-top jar, then spoon over the salad.

Scatter over chives, then cover salad and refrigerate for at least 1 hour before serving. Garnish with mixed herbs. *Serves 4-6*

VARIATION: Sprinkle tomatoes with finely chopped spring onion or shredded [illegible]

BASIL & TOMATO MAYONNAISE

3 tomatoes
8 teaspoons finely chopped fresh basil leaves
1 clove garlic, crushed
3 teaspoons snipped fresh chives
1 teaspoon caster sugar
155 ml (5 fl oz/ 2/3 cup) mayonnaise
6 teaspoons strained Greek yogurt

Put tomatoes in a bowl, cover with boiling water and leave for 1 minute, then drain and peel. Halve tomatoes and remove seeds.

Finely chop tomatoes, then put in a bowl with basil leaves.

Add garlic, chives and sugar and stir together using a wooden spoon. Stir in mayonnaise and yogurt until all ingredients are evenly blended. Cover with plastic wrap and chill until required.

Use to coat pasta or rice for a salad base. Serve as an accompaniment to lamb or chicken kebabs, or use to toss cooked mixed vegetables. *Serves 4*

LOBSTER FILO PARCELS

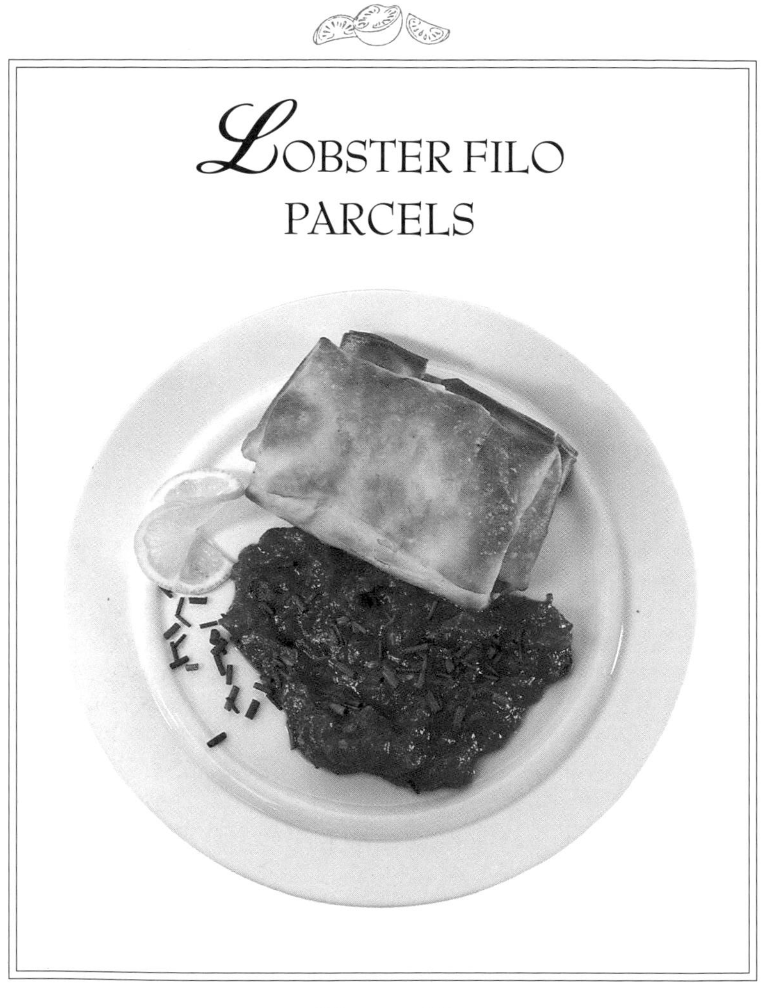

60 g (2 oz) butter
2 tablespoons chopped watercress
salt and pepper, to taste
185 g (6 oz) lobster meat, roughly chopped
8 sheets filo pastry
melted butter for brushing
500 g (1 lb) ripe tomatoes, skinned and seeded
1 teaspoon tomato purée (paste)
pinch of sugar
8-10 basil leaves
snipped chives and lemon twists, to garnish

Preheat oven to 200C (400F/Gas 6). In a bowl, blend together butter, watercress, and salt and pepper. Brush one sheet of filo pastry with melted butter; fold in half and brush again. Put a little lobster meat near one short edge and spread with butter. Roll up pastry, tucking in the ends. Make 4 parcels and place on a greased baking sheet, brushing with melted butter. Bake for 15 minutes, until golden. To make sauce, chop tomatoes. Put in a saucepan with tomato purée (paste), sugar, and salt and pepper; simmer for about 15-20 minutes. Tear basil leaves roughly and stir into sauce. Arrange 2 lobster parcels and a little tomato sauce on each serving plate and sprinkle chives over sauce. Garnish with lemon twists. *Serves 4*

CHEESY STUFFED TOMATOES

8 tomatoes
2 tablespoons vegetable oil
1 small onion, finely chopped
1 clove garlic, crushed
2.5 cm (1 in) piece fresh root ginger, grated
1 teaspoon ground cumin
½ teaspoon turmeric
½ teaspoon cayenne pepper
2 teaspoons ground coriander
salt
125 g (4 oz/½ cup) natural fromage frais
30 g (1 oz/¼ cup) Cheddar cheese, grated
1 tablespoon chopped fresh coriander, to garnish

Cut a slice from the top of each tomato. Scoop out centres, discard seeds, chop pulp and reserve. Drain on kitchen paper. Heat oil in a small frying pan, add onion and fry for 5 minutes, until soft. Stir in garlic and ginger and fry for 1 minute. Stir in remaining spices. Season and fry for 1 minute more. Stir in tomato pulp and cook for about 5 minutes, until thick. Preheat oven to 190C (375F/Gas 5). Stir fromage frais and half the Cheddar into spice mixture and spoon into tomato shells. Top with remaining Cheddar. Bake for 10-15 minutes. Sprinkle with coriander and serve hot. *Serves 4*

PICKLED MIXED VEGETABLES

1 cucumber, peeled
8 courgettes (zucchini), trimmed
500 g (1 lb) pickling onions, peeled
500 g (1 lb) red and green peppers (capsicums), seeded
500 g (1 lb) green or red tomatoes, skinned and seeded
9 teaspoons salt
315 g (10 oz/2 cups) light soft brown sugar
1 teaspoon celery seeds
1 teaspoon ground turmeric
1 teaspoon ground mace
4 teaspoons mustard seeds
625 ml (20 fl oz/2½ cups) wine vinegar

Cut all vegetables into thin slices and arrange in a large bowl, sprinkling salt between each layer. Cover with plastic wrap and leave in a cool place for 3 hours. Drain vegetables and rinse thoroughly under running water; drain thoroughly. To make spiced vinegar, place all ingredients in a stainless steel or enamel saucepan and stir over a gentle heat until sugar has dissolved; boil for 3 minutes. Add vegetables to vinegar, bring to boil, stirring occasionally. Cook for 1 minute. Spoon vegetables into clean hot jars until packed tightly. Fill to top with vinegar mixture and seal immediately with vinegar-proof, airtight lids. *Makes 2.5 kg (5 lb)*

TOMATO KUCHUMBER

375 g (12 oz) cherry tomatoes
6 spring onions
1 green chilli, seeded and chopped
3 teaspoons lemon juice
2 tablespoons chopped fresh coriander
salt and cayenne pepper
spring onion tassels, to garnish, if desired

Quarter the cherry tomatoes and arrange them in a serving bowl.

Cut spring onions diagonally into long, thin slices. Scatter onions and chilli over tomatoes and gently mix together.

Sprinkle vegetables with lemon juice and coriander and season with salt and cayenne pepper, then cover and chill for 30 minutes. Serve chilled, garnished with spring onion tassels, if desired. *Serves 4-6*

VARIATION: Use larger tomatoes, if preferred: slice thinly and arrange on a serving plate. Scatter other ingredients over top before chilling.

POTTERS RED RELISH

4 large ripe tomatoes
1 small red pepper (capsicum), seeded
1 small green pepper (capsicum), seeded
1 large onion
2 teaspoons salt
90 g (3 oz/½ cup) dark soft brown sugar
155 ml (5 fl oz/⅔ cup) malt vinegar
½ teaspoon sweet paprika
parsley, to garnish

Peel tomatoes and finely chop. Very finely chop red and green peppers (capsicums) and onion.

Put all the ingredients, except the garnish, into a heavy-based saucepan. Bring to boil, then reduce heat and simmer gently, stirring frequently for 1 hour or until mixture is thick.

Pour into a large jam jar, cover with a waxed disc and jam pot. Cover and leave for 1-2 weeks before using. Serve in a bowl, garnished with parsley. *Makes about 500 g (1 lb)*

NOTE: This spicy relish is delicious served with meat and game.

MUSSELS WITH TWO SAUCES

2 kg (4 lb) mussels in shell, cleaned
125 ml (4 fl oz/½ cup) dry white wine
TOMATO BASIL SAUCE
397 g (14 oz) can chopped tomatoes
1 tablespoon tomato purée (paste)
2 teaspoons torn basil leaves
1 teaspoon chopped oregano
pinch of sugar
salt and pepper, to taste
FENNEL SAUCE
30 g (1 oz) butter
1 leek, finely chopped
1 fennel bulb, finely chopped
60 ml (2 fl oz/¼ cup) double (thick) cream

Put mussels and wine in a large saucepan, cover and cook over a high heat, shaking pan, for 4-6 minutes. Drain, discarding any closed mussels and empty shells. Keep warm. To make tomato basil sauce, put all the ingredients in a saucepan and simmer for 15 minutes, until thickened and smooth. To make fennel sauce, in a pan melt butter, add leek and fennel, cover and cook for about 5 minutes, until softened. Add cream, season and simmer for 2 minutes. Purée. Fill mussel shells with the two sauces. *Serves 4-6*

TUNA & BASIL TOMATOES

4 medium beef tomatoes
salt and pepper
four 2.5 cm (1 in) thick slices white bread
90 g (3 oz/⅓ cup) garlic and herb butter
185 g (6 oz) can tuna chunks, drained
6 teaspoons breadcrumbs
1 teaspoon bottled pesto sauce
1 egg, separated
1 teaspoon finely grated Parmesan cheese
basil sprigs, to garnish

Preheat the oven to 200C (400F/Gas 6). Cut tops off tomatoes and hollow out tomato flesh. Season the insides of the tomatoes, then turn upside down to drain. Remove crusts from the bread then, using a 5 cm (2 in) pastry cutter, cut a hole in the centre of each slice. Melt 60 g (2 oz/¼ cup) of the flavoured butter and brush over both sides of each slice of bread. Melt remaining 30g (1 oz/6 teaspoons) butter and stir in tuna, breadcrumbs and pesto sauce. Whisk egg white until stiff. Stir egg yolk into the tuna mixture and fold in egg white.

Place the tomatoes in the holes in the bread and fill with tuna mixture. Sprinkle with parmesan cheese and bake for 12-15 minutes. Garnish and serve. *Serves 4*